Learn - Color - Write
First English Words

For Ukrainian Kids

This book belongs to

....

Color the word	Trace the word
hug	hug

Find and circle the word

He hugged me	think with Hug
Hug me more	hugged
Father hugging his daughter	hugging for cook

Understand the word

I hug my mom

Write the word in a sentence

Hug **me tight**

Color the word	Trace the word
you	you

Find and circle the word

You are a student
 	
Next to you
 	
We will go with you
	you yes
	             you
	     can
	you
	       no one

Understand the word

You are my best friend

Write the word in a sentence

Do you **want to play with us**

Color the word	Trace the word
can	⣏⣏⣏ ⣌⣏⣞

Find and circle the word

I can do it
 	
 Can i sit
 	
 Can Sam come over?
	can eat
	
	           go
	
	      can
	
	 can about
	     ask

Understand the word

You can do it

Write the word in a sentence

⣌⣏⣞ **I go out**

Color the word	Trace the word
cook	cook

Find and circle the word

Won't he cook?

I can cook

Alen is cooking

two   yes

              cook

        can

Cooking   for

        cook

Understand the word

I cook

Write the word in a sentence

Sam cooks **his favorite dish**

Color the word	Trace the word
think	think

Find and circle the word

I think healthy food is important to health	think with
	think
I think the internet has a few downsides	can
I think there are some errors	think for
	cook

Understand the word

I think it's a good idea

Write the word in a sentence

I  **it's a nice book**

Color the word	Trace the word
Î	i

Find and circle the word

I speak english	I above
	last
I went to the market	no
I am hungry	if
	I I

Understand the word

I am eating

Write the word in a sentence

I'm traveling to the village

Color the word	Trace the word
act	Act

Find and circle the word

Act normally until you find the opportunity	Act with Hug
Act like you	can
Act of service	Act cook Act

Understand the word

Act like a nurse

Write the word in a sentence

Act **right**

Color the word	Trace the word
run	run

Find and circle the word

Run away	run with
	run
Run out of petrol	can
Run in the garden	Act Act
	run

Understand the word

Run out of money   **I run**

Write the word in a sentence

Run **out of time**

Color the word	Trace the word
drink	drink

Find and circle the word

He drinks water	Act	with
		drinks
he drinks milk	drinks	
She drinks juice	drinks	Act
	cook	

Understand the word

I drink

Write the word in a sentence

I drink coffee

Color the word	Trace the word
give	give

Find and circle the word

I give you

I give a promise

I give you the money

Act   with   give

give

drinks   cook   give

Understand the word

I give you a book

Write the word in a sentence

I give

Color the word	Trace the word
study	study

Find and circle the word

Study time
 	
I study at the University of manchester
 	
I'm studying English
	study **with**
	          give
	    study
	          studying
	drinks **cook**

Understand the word

I study

Write the word in a sentence

I study **at school in Spanish**

Color the word	Trace the word
watch	watch

Find and circle the word

Watch the clock

Watch your language

You need to watch him - he's a strange

Watch   with

              Watch

    study

Watch   studying

      cook

Understand the word

I watch tv

Write the word in a sentence

Watch **this space**

Color the word	Trace the word
approve	approve

Find and circle the word

She doesn't approve of my friends

I wish my mother approved of my friends

I don't approve of that kind of language

approved   with

approve   approve

Watch   studying   cook

Understand the word

My request has been approved

Write the word in a sentence

He doesn't approve of smoking

Color the word	Trace the word
dream	dream

Find and circle the word

I often dream about flying.

I dream of living on a tropical island.

It was his dream to be a football player

dream   with   dream

approve

Watch   cook   dream

Understand the word

I dream of...

Write the word in a sentence

Someone would not dream of doing something

Color the word	Trace the word
sew	sew

Find and circle the word

My grandmother taught me to sew	sew with sew
Do you like to sew?	approve
She sewed her outfit by hand	sewed cook studying

Understand the word

She sews all her children's clothes

Write the word in a sentence

I had to sew up a hole in my jeans.

Color the word	Trace the word
fly	f̶l̶y̶

Find and circle the word

We watched a flock of birds fly over the fiel

A swarm of bees flew into the garden

We enjoy watching the birds fly over the water

fly   with
                    fly
        flew
                    studying
sewed   cook

Understand the word

Birds fly in the sky

Write the word in a sentence

There isn't really enough wind to f̶l̶y̶ **a kite today.**

Color the word	Trace the word
solve	solve

Find and circle the word

To solve a problem	solve with solve
Wars never solve anything	flew
Shouting won't solve anything	sewed solve cook

Understand the word

We solved the puzzle

Write the word in a sentence

The police are still no nearer to solving **the crime**

Color the word	Trace the word
walk	walk

Find and circle the word

I walk to work every morning

You can walk it in half an hour

I walked home

walk   with

                    solve

        flew

walk   walked

        cook

Understand the word

I walk ...

Write the word in a sentence

She walks **the dog for an hour every afternoon.**

Color the word	Trace the word
jump	jump

Find and circle the word

A parachute jump	walk jumped
	solve
The cats jumped up onto the table	flew
Can you jump this fence?	jump
	jump cook

Understand the word

I jump

Write the word in a sentence

The cats jumped up onto the table.

Color the word	Trace the word
answer	answer

Find and circle the word

There's no easy answer to the problem

I phoned last night but nobody answered

I think I got most of the answers right on the exam

walk   jumped

solve

answered

answers   answer

cook

Understand the word

I don't know the answer

Write the word in a sentence

I answered *the question*

Color the word	Trace the word
clap	clap

Find and circle the word

People will clap at the end of a speech
 	
She clapped her hands to call the dog in
 	
Everyone was clapping and cheering
	clapping **jumped**
	
	                                            solve
	
	               answer
	
	clapped **clap**
	               cook

Understand the word

I clap my hands

Write the word in a sentence

"When I clap **my hands, you stand still," said the teacher.**

Color the word	Trace the word
win	win

Find and circle the word

She would do anything to win his love

Did they win last night?

Our team won the game!

win   jumped   win   answer   won   cook   clap

Understand the word

I won the cup

Write the word in a sentence

Brazil are favourites to win this year's World Cup

Color the word	Trace the word
write	write

Find and circle the word

She writes children's books

Please write your name on the dotted line.

He writes well and is always a pleasure to read

writes   jumped

win

write

writes

won   cook

Understand the word

I write...

Write the word in a sentence

To write **a poem**

Color the word	Trace the word
sleep	sleep

Find and circle the word

She fell into a lovely deep sleep	writes sleep win
I was too excited to sleep much that night	sleep
I couldn't sleep because of all the noise next door	won cook sleep

Understand the word

I sleep...

Write the word in a sentence

Sleep **tight - see you in the morning.**

Color the word	Trace the word
close	close

Find and circle the word

The museum closes at 5.30

She closed the meeting with a short speech

The factory closed over ten years ago

closes   no

win

sleep

closed   closed

cook

Understand the word

She closes the door

Write the word in a sentence

I closed that bank account when I came to London

Color the word	Trace the word
plan	plan

Find and circle the word

Holiday plans	break no
	plans
What are your plans for this weekend?	plans
Events of this type rarely go according to plan	plan about cook

Understand the word

I plan...

Write the word in a sentence

She helped them to plan their route

Color the word	Trace the word
smell	smell

Find and circle the word

My hands smell of onions

That cake smells good

You smell lovely - what's your perfume?

smell   no   smell

plans

smells   cook   about

Understand the word

These socks smell foul!

Write the word in a sentence

This milk smells **funny**

Color the word	Trace the word
dance	dance

Find and circle the word

Can you dance the tango?

He was too shy to ask her to dance with him

Who was she dancing with at the party?

break   no

dance

dance

plan   about

dancing

Understand the word

I am dancing

Write the word in a sentence

Do you take dance lessons?

Color the word	Trace the word
buy	buy

Find and circle the word

I need to buy some new shoes

She was saving to buy a car.

We always buy paper from the same supplier

buy   no

buy

dance

plan   about

buy

Understand the word

She is buying a new car

Write the word in a sentence

This jacket is a really good buy

Color the word	Trace the word
cut	cut

Find and circle the word

Cut the meat up into small pieces	Cut Cut
	buy
This knife doesn't cut very well.	dance
Where did you have your hair cut?	plan about
	Cut

Understand the word

The barber cut my hair

Write the word in a sentence

Cut **the apple in half**

Color the word	Trace the word
see	see

Find and circle the word

Turn the light on so I can see

I can see you!

Her friends saw her home.

see   saw

                    buy

          dance

see   about

          Cut

Understand the word

I see

Write the word in a sentence

I can see for miles from up here

Color the word	Trace the word
enter	enter

Find and circle the word

She saw him enter the room.	enter saw buy
Please knock before entering	dance
The project is entering its final stages	entering entering about

Understand the word

They entered into the classroom

Write the word in a sentence

You have to enter password to access the database

Color the word	Trace the word
cry	cry

Find and circle the word

"don't cry," she said.	cry saw
She skinned her knee and began to cry	cry
She cried out in pain as she fell	dance
	cried about
	climbs

Understand the word

she is crying

Write the word in a sentence

She cried bitter tears when she got the letter.

Color the word	Trace the word
climb	climb

Find and circle the word

To climb the stairs	climbed saw
	climb
They climbed into the truck and drove away	dance
I've made three climbs so far this year.	entering about
	climbs

Understand the word

Climb to the top of the hill

Write the word in a sentence

To  **the mountain**

Color the word	Trace the word
build	build

Find and circle the word

Without a plan, you can't build a house

Some owls had built a nest in the chimney

We decided to build on high ground, above the river

built   saw   build   dance   build   climbs   about

Understand the word

Construction worker built a wall

Write the word in a sentence

He moved to London where he built up a successful career

Color the word	Trace the word
Complete	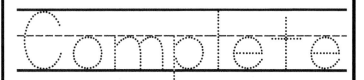

Find and circle the word

Her family completed the list of guests	completed saw
	complete
I *need two more cards to complete the set*	dance
Complete the sentence with one of the adjectives provided	complete about climbs

Understand the word

Project completed

Write the word in a sentence

The baby completed **our family**

Color the word	Trace the word
laugh	laugh

Find and circle the word

I couldn't stop laughing
 	
They laughed at her jokes.
 	
I laughed till I cried.
	laughed saw
	
	              laughed
	
	      dance
	
	complete laughing
	        climbs

Understand the word

I laughed

Write the word in a sentence

That guy always makes me

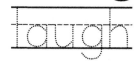

Color the word	Trace the word
draw	draw

Find and circle the word

Sam *can draw very well*

Anna drew an elephant

Draw a line at the bottom of the page

draw   saw

     draw

dance

complete   drew

    climbs

Understand the word

I draw

Write the word in a sentence

The children drew pictures of their families.

Color the word	Trace the word
talk	talk

Find and circle the word

My little girl has just started to talk	talk saw talk
The two sides have agreed to talk	dance
Talk won't get us anywhere	talk climbs drew

Understand the word

I had a talk with my boss

Write the word in a sentence

I've heard talk of a layoff

Color the word	Trace the word
read	read

Find and circle the word

She read slowly and quietly

It's not brilliant but it's worth a read

I read the book over the weekend.

read   saw
                    read
        read

   talk   drew
          climbs

Understand the word

I read...

Write the word in a sentence

She couldn't read **or write**

Color the word	Trace the word
listen	listen

Find and circle the word

What kind of music do you listen to?
 	
You haven't listened to a word I've said!
 	
Listen to this
	Listen saw
	             listened
	     read
	
	    listen drew
	         climbs

Understand the word

I listen...

Write the word in a sentence

Have a listen to this! I've never heard anything like it before

Color the word	Trace the word
play	play

Find and circle the word

He learned to play the clarinet	play saw
	played
The ball had gone out of play	read
She played the ace of spades	drew
	play climbs

Understand the word

I play football

Write the word in a sentence

Which team do you play for?

Color the word	Trace the word
touch	touch

Find and circle the word

Don't touch the machine when it's in use

That paint is wet, so don't touch

She can't touch the fire

touch   saw

touch

read

play   touch

climbs

Understand the word

I touch the leaf

Write the word in a sentence

Push the bookcases together until they touch

Color the word	Trace the word
wait	wait

Find and circle the word

We need to wait in line for the tickets

Wait here for me – I'll be back in a minute

The dentist kept me waiting for ages

touch   saw

wait

waiting

play   wait

climbs

Understand the word

I'm waiting for the bus

Write the word in a sentence

An envelope was waiting **for me when I got home.**

Color the word	Trace the word
open	open

Find and circle the word

You left the container open	open saw
	open
Someone had left the window wide open	waiting
The supermarket is open till 8.00 p.m	open
	play climbs

Understand the word

I opened the window

Write the word in a sentence

Make sure you have both files open at the same time.

Color the word	Trace the word
exit	exit

Find and circle the word

The character exits stage right

Click here to save and exit

Remember to save your work before you exit

exits   saw

      open

waiting

exit   exit

   climbs

Understand the word

I exited the building

Write the word in a sentence

Remember to save your work before you exit

Color the word	Trace the word
eat	eat

Find and circle the word

What do you want to eat for lunch?

We usually eat at about 7 p.m.

Do you eat meat?

eat   saw

          eat

    waiting

exit   eat

    climbs

Understand the word

I eat...

Write the word in a sentence

She eats **pizza**

Color the word	Trace the word
find	find

Find and circle the word

I couldn't find Alan's phone number.
 	
Vitamin C is found in citrus fruit.
 	
I had a map but I still couldn't find my way back to the hotel.
	find saw
	        find
	waiting
	exit found
	   climbs

Understand the word

I found a masterpiece

Write the word in a sentence

She doesn't find it easy to talk about her problems

Color the word	Trace the word
carry	carry

Find and circle the word

Would you like me to carry your bag for you?

These books are too heavy for me to carry

we were able to carry it onto the car

carry   saw

         carry

    waiting

exit   carry

    climbs

Understand the word

I carry...

Write the word in a sentence

Would you like to carry my bag?

Printed in Great Britain
by Amazon

81353594R00059